Creative Art Concepts for papercrafts

AN EFFORTLESS APPROACH TO FINE ART TECHNIQUES

Lea C...

C&T PUBLISHING

Text © 2007 Lea Cioci

Artwork © 2007 C&T Publishing, Inc.

Publisher: Amy Marson

Editorial Director: Gailen Runge

Acquisitions Editor: Jan Grigsby

Editor: Stacy Chamness

Book Designer: Jill K. Berry

Cover Designer: Kristy Zacharias

Production Coordinator: Matt Allen

Illustrator: Tim Manibusan

Copyeditor/Proofreader: Wordfirm Inc.

Photography: C&T Publishing, Inc., unless otherwise noted

Published by C&T Publishing, Inc., P.O. Box 1456, Lafayette, CA 94549

Attention Teachers: C&T Publishing, Inc., encourages you to use this book as a text for teaching. Contact us at 800-284-1114 or www.ctpub.com for more information about the C&T Teachers Program.

We take great care to ensure that the information included in our books is accurate and presented in good faith, but no warranty is provided nor are results guaranteed. Having no control over the choices of materials or procedures used, neither the author nor C&T Publishing, Inc., shall have any liability to any person or entity with respect to any loss or damage caused directly or indirectly by the information contained in this book. For your convenience, we post an up-to-date listing of corrections on our website (www.ctpub.com). If a correction is not already noted, please contact our customer service department at ctinfo@ctpub.com or at P.O. Box 1456, Lafayette, CA 94549.

Trademark (™) and registered trademark (®) names are used throughout this book. Rather than use the symbols with every occurrence of a trademark or registered trademark name, we are using the names only in the editorial fashion and to the benefit of the owner, with no intention of infringement.

Library of Congress Cataloging-in-Publication Data

Cioci, Lea.
  Creative art concepts for papercrafts : an effortless approach to fine art techniques / Lea Cioci.
      p. cm.
  ISBN-13: 978-1-57120-402-8 (paper trade : alk. paper)
  ISBN-10: 1-57120-402-4 (paper trade : alk. paper)
  1. Paper work. 2. Handicraft. I. Title.

TT870.C576 2007
745.54–dc22

                            2006021835

Printed in China

10 9 8 7 6 5 4 3 2 1

Contents

Acknowledgments

I would like to thank the entire staff of C&T Publishing for being patient and helpful through this process of putting my art and techniques into book form.

Special thanks go out to Jan Grigsby and Amy Marson of C&T Publishing for using my artwork in other C&T books and believing in the vision that my art represents: personal expression of self.

I would also like to thank C&T's Stacy Chamness, who edited, added input, and assisted me with all the technical aspects of making this book a reality. Stacy, your upbeat personality and expertise are things I admire, and they helped us through the small challenges that arose. Thank you, Stacy!

Next, I must thank the following individuals:

- My husband, Al, and my daughter, Karissa—unique individuals who sparkle with sunshine and love. They've supported me all the way with encouragement and pride as I've pursued my dreams.

- My son, Spencer—a cartooning talent who has created altered book pages. I needed someone to do the basic hand shots, showing how I wanted the final shots to be photographed. He spent a lot of time holding ink, brushing, and pretending he was creating art. Spence, I couldn't have gotten it done without you!

- The artists who have contributed to the galleries—people I've known for years, whose art inspires and touches me deeply. Thank you for sharing your personal expressions reflecting my techniques!

- The manufacturers whose products I use day in and day out—products that I believe in and love to design with.

Lastly, I thank the infinite powers that be, for bringing forth beauty we can all touch and feel.

Dedication

I dedicate this book to the vibrant paintings of my father, who passed away on May 23, 2005. Without his love and passion for painting and architectural drawings, I might never have started this journey of expressing my passion through art.

I would also like to dedicate this book to the memory of Cathy Mace, who, together with her husband, Richard, owned the highly prolific paper company Papers by Catherine. Cathy inspired me on so many levels. She was bright, funny, and the consummate business professional. She showed me techniques that motivated me to create books and intricate fold projects. Although Cathy's style of art was different than mine, she liked my freeform, whimsical, artsy way of expression. I will greatly miss Cathy's laugh, talents, and spirit.

Introduction

What is an artist? Many people say, "I'm not an artist, but I'd like to be one." An artist is anyone who loves to play with art materials, expressing his or her true nature. The representation ends up as a beautiful piece of artwork.

I've had a passion for art from the time I was little. As strange as it may seem, my start came from reading *MAD* magazine and copying some of the drawings in ink. I moved on to paints and tissue with collage as the age of Peter Max and psychedelic art abounded. I am obsessed with color and texture!

My creative expressions are freeform, although buried deep within my brain are the lessons about color and design that I learned in art school. When first working with rubber stamps I found that most of the finished works I saw were simply stamped, cut out, and layered. Susan P. Rothamel of USArtQuest inspired me to incorporate my fine arts knowledge into my stamp art, and to be free in my expressions. Mica powder and UTEE (Ultra Thick Embossing Powder), along with collage stamp images, helped me feel comfortable in my artistic skin. Painting and experimental ways of working with media combined to let me define me!

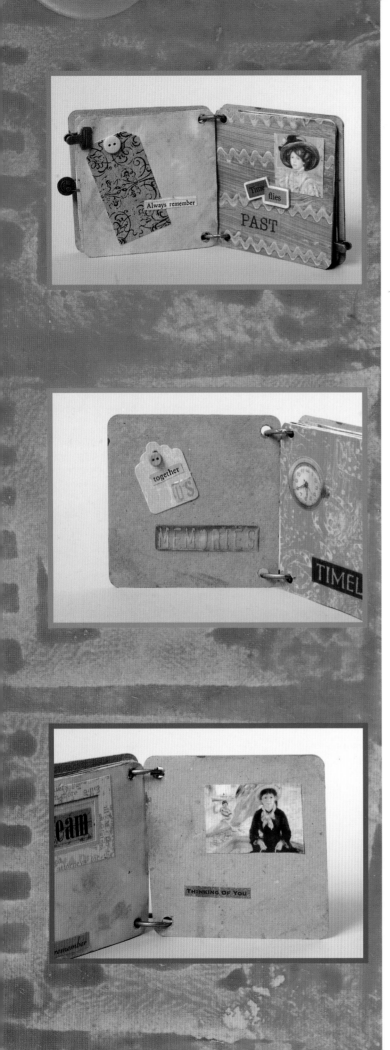

This book will guide you through many techniques that have no set finished result in many regards. It is all about taking the basic ways of working with these media and creating the art that expresses you. The only area of real study relates to shading with pastel pencils to give a realistic look to stamped images. Guides to the basics of color and design can be found starting on page 72. The knowledge imparted will help you communicate through your art on a level you might have never dreamed of before!

Wherever you are in your journey, know that you are truly, really an artist! The desire to grow and experiment is commendable. Never be afraid to try, explore, and experiment!

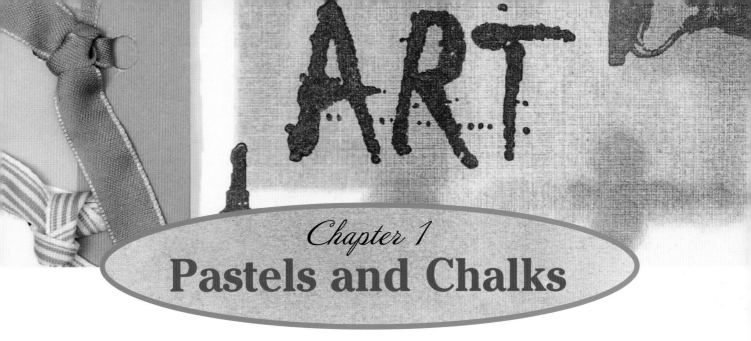

Chapter 1
Pastels and Chalks

Pastels are brilliant in color and high in pigmentation, providing concentrated color, and they are mixable with other media. The pure pigment applied to paper is an eye-catching way to get immediate design results. Pastels are easy to use because there is no drying time, although a spray fixative is required in many cases to set pastel powders. Oil pastels have a crayon-type consistency, are more permanent, and do not have to be set with a fixative (although there are oil-pastel fixatives available). The hardness and softness of a pastel depends on the amount of binder used. Soft pastels have less binder and contain more pigment. Hard pastels have less pigment and more binder.

Most paper types can be used, but for more dramatic results with rich color, papers with tooth or texture are better for bonding pastel color to the surface.

Pastel Pencils

Pastel pencils provide a controlled way of adding color and shading to your art. Most paper artists use them with rubber stamps. There are two ways of working with the pencils, One-Color Shade Out (page 8), using one color of pastel pencil, and Multiple-Color Overlay Shading (page 10). While One-Color Shade Out is the simplest method, Multiple-Color Overlay Shading brings striking multishaded dimension to your work. Once you learn where to put lights and darks, endless possibilities await you!

Craft stores offer a wide variety of pastel pencils at different price levels. Derwent pastel pencils are readily available and they are great-quality pencils for stamp art projects.

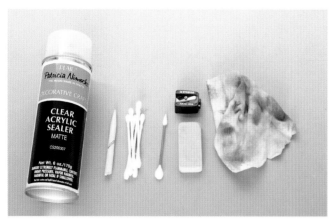

Basic Tools to Use With Pastels

Eraser—A nylon or kneaded eraser will pick up any finger smudges left on paper.

Blending tools—In the fine art world, blending stumps are used to soften the edges of pastel lines or to blend color gradations. In our world, cotton swabs will do the job! Cotton swabs come in many styles; I prefer the makeup-applicator style for this purpose.

Fixative—Spray-type matte fixative can be found in any craft store.

Sharpener—You will need a good pencil sharpener made for pastels. Pastel lead is soft and will break easily if you are not using a sharpener with a sharp blade.

Permanent inkpad—Permanent ink (in black or brown) is necessary to keep the image from smearing while you are applying pastels.

TIP I often use two blending tools— one for light colors and one for dark colors.

Outlined stamp images work best for the one-color shade out method.

Image on cream-colored paper

One-Color Shade Out

Highlights or shading indicate light or shadowed areas in your artwork. Most stamped work appears two-dimensional. By adding highlights and shadows to a base color, you can make the artwork look more realistic and appear more three-dimensional. For the One-Color Shade Out method, a single color of pastel pencil will do all the shading in an area!

1 Stamp an image with permanent ink.

2 Using pastels, apply color around the inside edges of the stamped image.

3 Using the blending tool of your choice, pull the pastel color from the inside edge toward the center of the image, using a circular motion. The color will fill smaller areas of the stamp, which is okay because they are often areas that would be shaded anyway.

TIP Areas that overlap need more pencil blending on the overlapped "bottom layer." For example, add more color "under" the top feathers to pop them out.

4 Spray the finished work lightly with 2 coats of matte fixative, from a distance of 8″ to 10″ away from the work.

The same image on white linen paper

Multiple-Color Overlay Shading

This technique is a beautiful way to show depth and dimension by using several layered colors, one at a time. The results are striking and realistic. Refer to the information above about shading. In my easy method, I use the base color, a highlight, and a shadow color or two. To get a more natural effect, I do not use black or white to highlight or shade. Occasionally I will use a smidgen of white as an accent on the highlight; however, I prefer colors such as yellow or light blue for highlights, and browns, deep blues, or greens for shadows. I am using a pear image to demonstrate this technique. You could use any stamp image or scenery stamp with appropriate colors in these same shades.

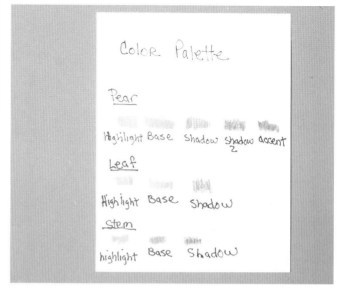

The palette

Many stamp images have little dots on them indicating where the shadows are, which is helpful when deciding where to highlight and shade.

> **TIP** Yellow textured cardstock was used to enhance the pear's coloring.

Additional Project Supplies

- Pastel pencils

- Russet Archival Ink and Tea Dye Distress Ink—Ranger

- Fasenator—EK Success

- Sticky Dots adhesive—Therm O Web

- Pear stamp—After Midnight Art Stamps

Scenic images and nature stamps look fabulous when used with this technique. The leaf and stem have only the highlight (lime or yellow-green), base color (green), and shadow (brown). An accent (red-orange) and secondary shadow (brown) are used to add further realism to the pear itself. Refer to the palette as you follow the next steps.

1 Stamp the image with permanent ink.

2 Highlight the appropriate areas, then blend the edges of the highlight with a blending tool.

> **TIP** To remove color from the blending tool, rub excess color off on a scrap piece of paper.

3 Lightly color the rest of the pear in the base color and blend into the highlight. Blend one color into the other using a blending stump or a cotton swab and a circular motion, moving the darker color to slightly overlap the lighter color. Work the color into the paper.

4 Add the highlight accent and blend in. Follow the steps above to highlight, add the base color and the shadow of the leaf and stem, and then blend all the colors.

5 Add shadows in the curves of the pear by the stem and where the front pear overlaps the back pear, and blend in. Use the lighter rust shadow color first, then the darker brown shadow color.

6 Add the shadows and the highlight accents where they would fall on the image. I finished the book cover design with ripped paper edged with ink, mounted on dark green cardstock, and added words and a charm.

> **TIP** To edge cardstock with ink, swipe the edge of the paper against an inkpad.

Art Chalks

I love playing with chalks! That is the word—play. Using chalk in **sticks** or from **trays** allows you to add color in a more liberated way. Chalk **powders** are softer and subtler on the paper, yet building up layers can deepen the colors to a greater intensity.

There are many ways to play with chalk powders. In scrapbooking, chalks are used to edge pages, shade die cuts, and decorate plain or patterned backgrounds. You can also use stencils to lay down color within a shape. Chalk powder works well on all porous surfaces—flat paper, cast pulp paper, paper clay, and even wood and modeling paste, stencil paste, or spackle.

Cast pulp paper is paper that has been ripped up, put in a blender with water, and then strained and pressed into a mold.

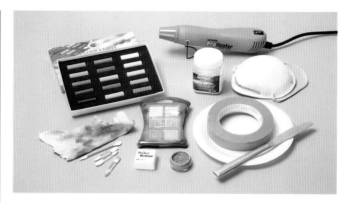

Basic Tools for Working With Chalks

■ Stick or tray chalks and mica powders (The softer the chalk, the easier it is to use.)

■ Knife to scrape powder from the chalk onto a palette

■ Foam plate for a palette

■ Perfect Medium—Ranger

■ Soft cloth and cotton swabs

■ Removable tape

■ Heat tool (to heat embossing powder)

■ Optional: Painter's mask

Additional Tools

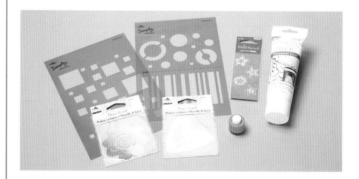

■ Stencils (brass or Mylar)

■ Modeling paste or spackle

■ Hole punches

WARNING:

Mica and chalk powders are safe to use; however, individuals with mica allergies, asthma, or chronic respiratory irritations need to be cautious while working with this medium. Simply use a painter's mask, available at any home improvement store.

Create a palette of chalk powder

1 Use a knife to scrape chalk onto the foam plate.

2 Pick up the chalk powder with a soft cloth and use a circular motion to rub chalk onto the surface you wish to color.

3 To add another color and blend, pick up another chalk powder color on a clean area of the cloth and overlap one color onto the other. The goal is to blend the colors at the point they meet until you can't tell where one color ends and the other begins.

TIP Two overlapping colors will either blend into a third color, or the darker color will take over. Refer to the section in the back of the book on color and color themes (pages 72–77) to guide you if you get stuck.

Stencils

Stencil squares used for a background. Blend several colors of chalk powder, using stencils or another edging tool (such as ripped paper) as a mask.

TIP Work with light colors of chalk powder first. While dark colors will blend nicely over light colors, light colors get lost over dark colors. Build your design with the lighter colors, then use the darker colors for patterns and accents.

Blending With Stencils

1 Place the stencil on your paper.

2 Holding the stencil down, pick up chalk powder with a soft cloth and apply it as directed on page 13.

3 Overlap the squares, starting with the large square as the major focal point and adding smaller squares as accents.

TIP Use removable tape to secure the stencil to the paper to prevent it from slipping.

4 With darker or contrasting colors of chalk powder, add accents on and around the squares background. Use word stencils if words are to be added.

5 Spray seal your layout once you finish with the chalks and stencils, then stamp images on top.

T I P Create your own stencils using hole punches and die cuts! The frames that are left from punching or die cutting are perfect as stencils.

Chalk Popping

This is an easy technique that creates beautiful results! Use Ranger's Clear Resist, Ranger's Perfect Medium, or Tsukineko's VersaMark Watermark stamp pads. When chalk powders are added, the image magically "pops up." It is fun to blend several colors over the whole surface to give a tie-dyed look.

How-To

1 Stamp the image using one of the inks mentioned above.

2 Lightly set the ink with a heat tool by turning the tool on and moving it back and forth a few inches above the stamped image.

3 Pick up chalk powders and start blending colors on the surface, making the image pop.

Mini Travel Memories

Supplies

- 3″ × 3″ white blank board book—Create & Treasure
- Pastel pencils (A 24-pencil set works just fine!)
- Russet Archival Ink—Ranger
- All Night Media blending chalks—Plaid
- Kneaded eraser
- Sticky Dots adhesive—Therm O Web
- Scenic image stamp—The Artist's Stamp (Any image with trees and a hillside view will work.)
- Studio K Book Kit stickers—K&Company
- Mini scrapbook travel elements—Colorbök
- Ribbon brads—Karen Foster Design
- Awl to punch holes

How-To

1 Stamp the image with Archival ink.

2 Choose your color palette. To determine where highlights and shadows are, look at your stamped image and decide where the light is coming from (stamp the image on scratch paper to figure it out if you're not sure).

3 Start with the sky and put down the highlights. I don't normally use white, but because we are working with clouds, we will use both white and lime green as highlights. Color white over the whole sky area and blend in the chalk. Referring to the illustration, add a little lime green in the center and mid-bottom right and upper left. Blend light blue as the base color around the highlighted areas. Add dark blue to the lower half of the sky where it is in the shadows.

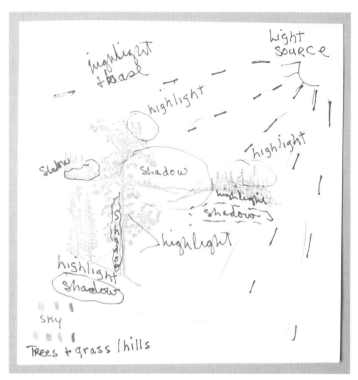

4 For the trees, blend lime green on the right side of the big tree and the smaller tree in the foreground of the stamped image. The trees in the background do not need much lime green because they don't get much light.

5 Next, use the grass green as the base for the leaves and blend slightly into the lime green on the front leaves.

6 Use olive green as the shadow and blend it on the left side of the leaves on the front trees, and underneath the leaves.

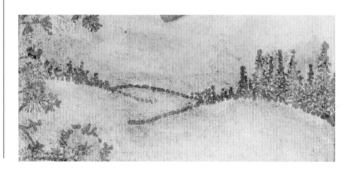

7 Blend the olive green on all the trees in the background.

8 For the bark of the front tree, blend a scant amount of lime green on the right side, and blend brown on the left. Use the brown pencil to go over the branches of the trees with short, sketchy lines.

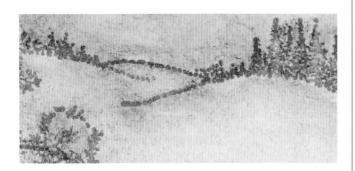

9 For the hills and grass, start with lime green and blend color on the bumps of the hill that stick out and will get the light.

10 Color the whole area with grass green and blend in.

11 Shade with the olive green behind where the hills overlap and behind the front trees, blending in.

12 Add brown to accentuate the shadows. Spray seal the cover when finished.

13 For each page of the book, use stencils and die-cut negatives to create patterns or just blend a solid color and edge with another color of chalk powder. Use stickers, die-cut quotes (edged with chalk powder), photos, and embellishments such as buttons, brad ribbons, and so on.

14 To finish the book, blend blue onto the back cover and olive green onto the edges, and spray seal.

Pamphlet-Stitch Card Journal

Supplies

- 5½″ × 8½″ piece of cardstock
- 3 pieces of copy paper, each 4″ × 8″
- A scrap of cream cardstock
- Coffee Bean and Cosmic Copper Brilliance inks—Tsukineko
- Aegean Blue VersaMagic ink—Tsukineko
- Blending chalks in assorted colors—Plaid
- *Ornament of Love* stamp—"Lila's Divine Play" from After Midnight Art Stamps
- *Thinking of You* sticker—K&Company
- *Adore* charm—All My Memories
- Paper clip—EK Success
- 22-gauge copper wire—Artistic Wire
- Sticky Dots adhesive—Therm O Web
- Round beads (plastic or glass)
- Awl

How-To

1 Using the blending chalks, make a palette of colors of your choice. I used teal, purple, orange, and lime green. Blend the chalks onto the cardstock and spray seal.

2 Stamp all the images except the squiggle design with Coffee Bean Brilliance ink on the scrap of cardstock. Stamp the squiggle in blue. Accent the images with chalk, and spray seal.

3 Rip the images out of the paper. Edge the woman and the squiggle with copper ink and edge the word *admire* with blue ink.

> **TIP** Make the clip copper to match the wire! Place the clip on paper and dab copper ink onto the clip until it is covered. Heat set it with the heat tool. Do not handle the clip until it has cooled!

4 Fold the 5½″ × 8½″ piece of cardstock in half, creating a 4¼″ × 5½″ cover.

5 Mount the images to the card front and add the sticker, word charm, and clip.

6 Fold the copy paper in half and fit it inside the cover.

> **TIP** Use graduated sizes of colored copy paper for interest!

7 Open the card and use an awl to punch a hole through all the layers of paper and the cover in the center of the fold. Measure about 1″ in from each edge and punch 2 more holes, so you have 3 holes down the center of the fold.

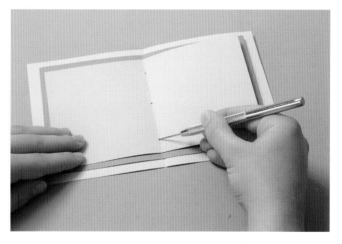

8 Push the wire through the top hole from the inside to the outside, then push the wire through the bottom hole from the outside to the inside.

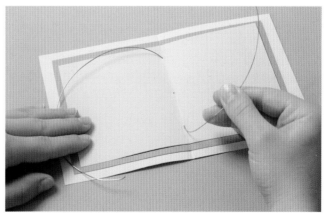

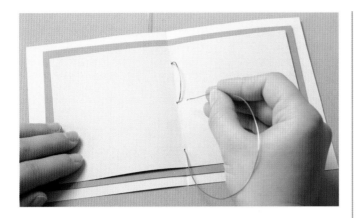

9 Both ends of the wire are now inside the card. Make sure the 2 ends are even and gently pull them tight. Push both ends through the center hole to the outside of the book. Gently pull them tight and twist the wire to secure it. Add beads by slipping them onto the wire and twisting the wire once or twice around the end bead. There will be some wire left over.

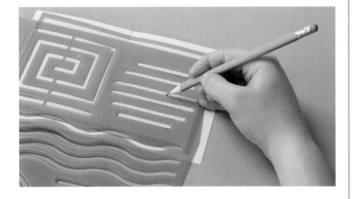

10 Stamp words inside the card, or create word lines with a stencil template.

TIP Twist the wire around a pencil (or your finger!) for an added decorative look.

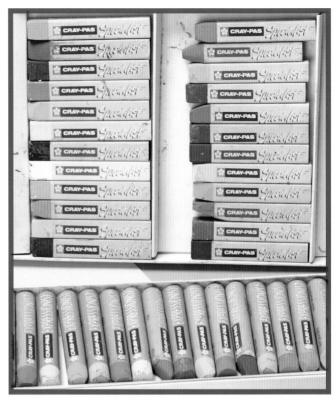

Oil Pastels

Oil pastels make rich and vibrant backgrounds for mixed-media artwork. Starting with an oil pastel background will enhance any paper art-work! Oil pastels are made of rich pigments with an oil binder. The softer the grade, the easier it is to spread the pastels. Most soft-grade oil pastels are reasonably priced, but there are more expensive brands that blend like butter, and the investment is well worth it.

My favorite oil pastels on the market are Sakura of America's Expressionist and Specialist oil pastels. The colors are vibrant, they are inexpensive, and they blend easily. I use the metallic Senniler oil pastels to add rich metallic accents. Senniler also makes an oil pastel fixative, which the company recommends using on finished art to prevent smudging.

I will mention mica powders here. These are cosmetic-grade powders with shimmer and shine that can be used with pastels or chalk powders or by themselves.

Supplies

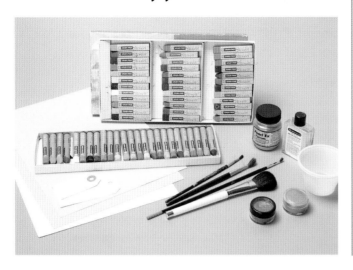

- Oil pastels
- Turpenoid
- Soft watercolor brushes
- Mica powders
- Smooth cardstock
- Tags
- Tag board
- Ancient Page ink—Clearsnap
- Rubber stamps (Those shown are from After Midnight Art Stamps.)
- Fibers—Fiber Scraps

Working With Oil Pastels

Overlap several stamped images to create a collage. Start with outlined images or images you want in the background, then add the bolder images to the foreground.

To create a simple background, I prefer a smooth cardstock. Mail tags or a tag board surface (sold at school supply stores) are excellent to work with.

This is a fun, messy technique because you use your fingers to spread the oil pastels. This is why it is important to have a soft grade of oil pastels! The oil in your fingers mixes with the oil binder in the pastel and helps the color spread out and move on the surface you are coloring. If you have chemical-sensitive skin you can put a bandage on your fingertip or cover your fingertip with plastic wrap; it'll still work.

Work with the oil pastels a little bit before you begin your project, to get the feel of them. This will help you learn how heavily to lay the color down.

Creating Backgrounds

1 Start by making a small, heavy patch of color on the cardstock surface. Rub your index finger over it quickly so it will spread out.

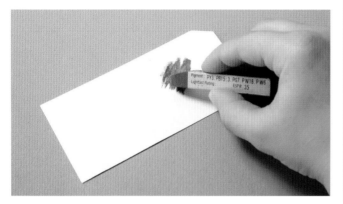

A small but heavy patch of color

TIP Change fingers if you use a darker color and then need to go back to a light color. This will prevent colors from turning muddy.

2 Add a second patch of color near the first color. Spread the second color, overlapping into the first color. Notice that the 2 overlapping colors mix together, creating a third color. See Chapter 5 (pages 72–75) for further color-mixing ideas.

3 Keep adding color, spreading and overlapping until the whole surface is filled with color.

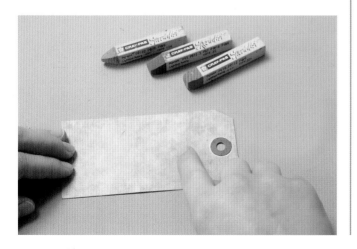

4 After the color is blended, I like to add mica powders for highlight accents. I often use a transparent gold, which covers the surface with a sheen. Putting mica powder on the surface helps seal the oils to make it easier to stamp on.

TIP To brush mica powder over the surface, place the tip of a soft, fluffy brush into the powder (a little goes a long way). Swirl the brush in the container cap and tap off the excess, then lightly brush the powder over the surface. Add more as needed—it is easier to add powder than to remove powder.

5 Use richer, inkier pads like Clearsnap's Ancient Page or Tsukineko's Brilliance and VersaFine inks to stamp on the surface. Let the inks set up for a minute.

Oil Pastel Watercolors

3 Brush over the patch of oil pastel color and watch the odorless paint thinner break down the pastel into a nice watercolor wash.

4 Keep adding colors, brushing the colors in together. You might want to use one brush for light colors and one for dark colors.

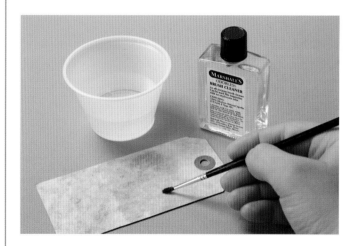

Stamp over the watercolor to create your design.

To create a watercolor look, I use an odorless paint thinner (usually found near oil paints in craft stores) with the oil pastels.

1 Lay a patch of color down as described in Creating Backgrounds (page 22). Pour a little paint thinner in a cup.

2 Dip a flat watercolor brush in the paint thinner. Tap any extra off on the edge of the cup and then on a paper towel. (You want the brush damp but not wet.)

TIP Another way to do this is to lay a small but heavy patch of color down on a scrap of paper, use the brush with thinner on it to pick up the color, and then brush it onto your surface.

Oil Pastel Fabric Rubbings

Close-up of angel goddess

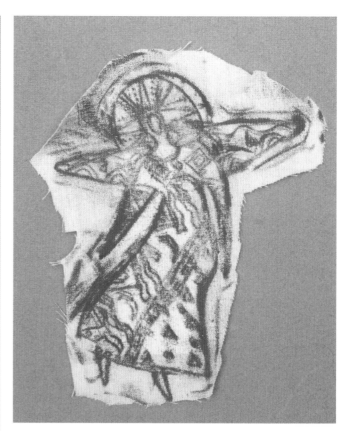

The rubbing before adhering it to another surface

TIP Once you have rubbed the stamp image on the material, add more color with different oil pastels!

I love this technique! You can create glorious works of art or gifts, quickly and easily. In elementary school we went around with paper and crayons and did rubbings on anything that had texture. I applied this method by doing stamp-image rubbings. I use muslin or T-shirt jersey—very thin fabric—to do this. Test your chosen fabrics to ensure that the image comes through well.

How-To

1 Place a stamp face up on your work surface.

2 Place a scrap of fabric (large enough to cover the stamp) over the image and hold the fabric taut (or secure it with masking tape).

3 Rub oil pastels over the wrapped stamp.

4 Unwrap the stamp and place the image on fusible web (I prefer HeatnBond Ultrahold Iron-on Adhesive), put a piece of scrap paper over the rubbing, and, following the manufacturer's instructions, iron the fusible web to the back of the rubbing. This not only turns your rubbing into an appliqué, it also removes the waxy binder from the pastels, leaving only the beautiful color. To attach the piece to a shirt, a bag, cardstock, an altered book, or any other such object, simply peel the backing from the web and iron the piece onto the surface!

5 Rub spots of coordinating colors onto the background. I used copper metallic oil pastel to accent my page, and brushed mica powder in various colors over the background using coordinating colors (for example, I used gold mica powder in the yellow area).

An altered book page with an appliqué-stitched rubbing ironed onto the page. Note the pocket!

6 A little pocket was created by ripping out a page from the book, saving the upper right corner of the page (triangular shape) and flipping it to fit the lower left corner. I took a mauve pastel from my palette and rubbed it in, adding a little pink oil pastel, and then edged the whole pocket with metallic copper oil pastel, accenting it with mica powder. I used a Therm O Web Memory Tape Runner (Sources, page 78) on the 2 straight edges, so the ripped edge is open for the pocket. Again, I used iron-on adhesive to attach the image to the background.

[A]n authentic life is the most personal form of worship.

Sarah Ban Breathnach

WISH

DAYS
LIKE THESE

Self

Take joy
in the pleasures
time can bring

authentic

ect Harmony

A

inward
journey

Self

Gallery

Sun card by Shari Myers.

Chalking works on many surfaces.

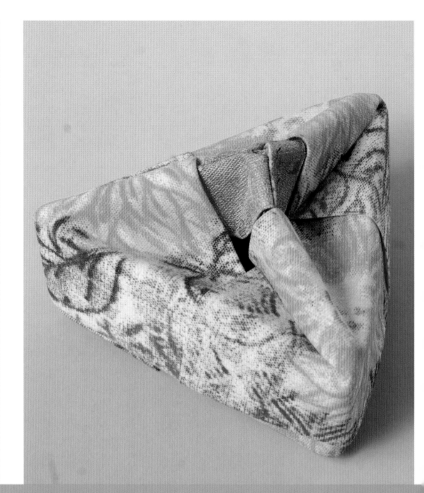

Above: Shari Myers used the embossing "pop out" technique with chalk.

Below: Puff embossing powder gives the image texture.

Above: Jeannette Stumpfel did an oil pastel rubbing, but after ironing the fabric she did the rubbing again to make the outline stand out more.

Below: The leaf was cast by placing a stamp face up and adding layers of toilet paper, wet with a soft brush. Once the paper was dry, the casting was lifted and the piece was trimmed with scissors and colored with chalks.

Above: The tag backgrounds were all colored with blended oil pastels.

Below: The oil pastel rubbing was created on muslin then ironed onto a fabric bag.

Accenting die cuts and stickers is easy using chalk colors.

Watercolor paper was used and the background color was applied with a soft cloth.

Chapter 2
Mono Printing

With Rubber Stamps and Pigmented Paste

Mono printing is a method of paper decoration that involves creating a distinctive imprint by applying ink to a flat surface and transferring it to paper. Very bold prints are being made with the use of various tools and the imagination of the artist. These "tools" include anything and everything—from kitchen forks and hair picks to stamps and sponges. Most think of mono printing using just ink, but I prefer the "paste" method and like to make my own paper prints with solid and heavily outlined stamps. By applying paste to the surface and removing the paste with the stamp or tool, I create a "negative" mono print.

Printing With Paste

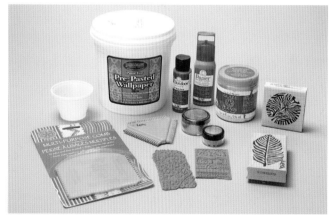

Materials and tools used for printing with pastes

When I first started to play with pastes, I bought powdered wallpaper paste, but there were lumps and the consistency of the paste wasn't as thick as I needed.

Experimenting more, I found that either premixed wallpaper paste or Plaid's neutral glaze were exactly what I was looking for! Both work well when you print into the paste with stamps.

Plaid's colored glazes and Papier paint, and LuminArte's Radiant Pearls paint and other pigmented media also work great. These take a longer time to dry than regular paint and lift off the page easily with tools and stamps.

Finished paste paper ready for projects

Creating Pigmented Paste

Wallpaper paste and Plaid's neutral glaze are clear—perfect if you want to add your own color to the base paste. Plaid's glaze does come in many colors, so if you feel uncomfortable mixing the colors, try these—they are ready to use right out of the container.

Pigments and paints add color to wallpaper paste or neutral glaze

TIP **Plaid's neutral glaze is not as gelatinous as wallpaper paste, so more pigment needs to be added to get the same consistency. Precolored Plaid glaze is gelatinous enough as is.**

Paints and pigments used to color the paste should be water-based. I like LuminArte's Primary Elements because the colors are so brilliant, rich, and shimmering. You can also use inexpensive poster paints, powdered pigments, or inkpad re-inkers.

Coloring Your Paste

1 Separate the paste into small containers and add 1 to 2 teaspoons of pigment color to the paste.

2 Mix until smooth. Make sure the paste is well mixed because lumps make for an unattractive design that is difficult to add pattern to. Also, keep in mind that the paste will dry darker than the wet paste color.

Creating Pigmented Paste Prints

Supplies

- Prepared pigmented paste
- Paper
- Foam brushes
- Glass, tile, or plastic sheet
- Drop cloth
- Baby wipes
- Paper towels
- Rubber stamps with heavy outlines

Patterns can be made with anything that can be pressed into the paste. There are many combing tools available at home improvement or craft stores. Other choices are forks, buttons, and so on.

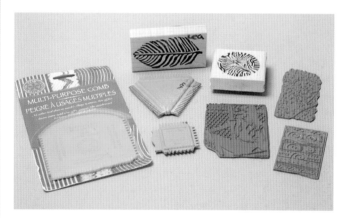

Tools that will leave a pattern in paste

Some stamp companies make great stamp images to use with this style of negative mono printing. See Sources on page 78.

How-To

Many artists like to start creating with paste paper by wetting the paper; however, I feel that if you get paste that is the right consistency, this is not necessary. I do not like to thin the paste down at all when working, but this is an option you might want to experiment with.

1 Cover your work surface with a drop cloth and then place a piece of glass, tile, or plastic on top of that. This creates a hard surface and ensures that the finished print doesn't stick and can be lifted easily to dry. Have paper towels and baby wipes available to clean your work area and stamps, and also a garbage can nearby so that you can discard the used paper towels and baby wipes. Printing can be messy, so use plastic gloves if you want.

2 To apply paste, use a foam brush and brush paste onto the paper. Coat the paper well. If the paper is large, work one area at a time, allowing for free play with printing and creating designs before the paste dries.

TIP If you work for several hours and the paste starts to thicken in the container, a couple of drops of water or neutral glaze can be added to keep the consistency stable.

3 Once the paste has been applied to the paper, press a stamp into the surface. You will see the reversed pattern of the stamp image. Wipe the stamp off after each use. This will prevent buildup on the stamp, which can make the impressions less clear.

TIP In addition to stamps, try dragging a combing tool in many directions through the paste to create patterns or leave an impression in the paste.

TIP If the image doesn't print well, the paste is too thick, the paste has dried too much, or the image you are using is not bold enough. The paste is forgiving . . . if the area has dried, just add more paste!

TIP Do not let the paste dry on the stamp; it will be hard to clean later on. Use baby wipes or a wet cloth to prevent this from happening. If stamps have paste stuck in the recesses of the image, use an old toothbrush to remove the stuck paste.

4 Once it dries, the paste print is ready to be used in art projects.

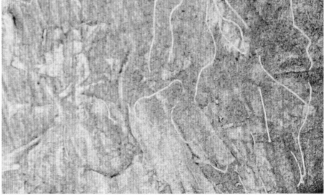

Enhancements Under and Over Pigmented Paste

Experiments with various media lead to endless ideas!

Brush on one color of paste, and then brush on another color of paste, letting them mix together as you brush. When you print with a stamp, you will have a multicolored print.

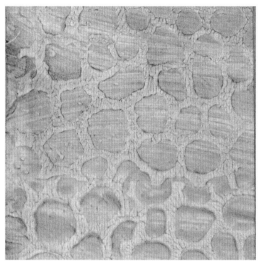

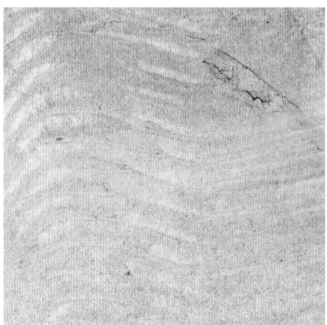

Mixing two-paste pigments on paper before mono printing

Brush one color of paste completely on the paper and let dry. Now brush another color of paste over the dried paste and print the paper with the stamp images. The color from below will show through where the paste was removed when you pressed the stamp into the paper.

Two-paste printing

Randomly paint watercolors or LuminArte's Twinkling H20s, which are shimmering watercolors (see Sources, page 78). Once the watercolors have dried, follow the same instructions for applying paste and printing. As in the other method, the watercolors will show through where the stamp removes paste.

LuminArte's Twinkling H20s underneath and paste on the surface

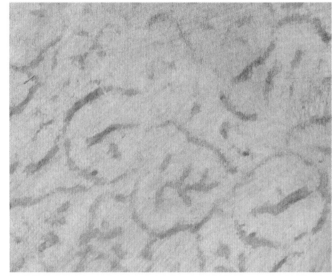

Create a resist by scribbling oil pastels before applying paste. Using a texture plate will give you exact patterns (Fiskars has some great texture plates; see Sources, page 78). When you brush the paste over the oil pastel patterns, the oil pastel will "resist" the paste and the colors will show through. When brushing the paste, pick up a small amount of paste rather than coating the paste heavily as before; lightly scrub the paste over the surface so the oil pastels can "pop" through the paste.

Add color to the open areas of the paste paper once it has dried. Watercolors, chalk, mica powder, and so on can be added to enhance the finished paste paper.

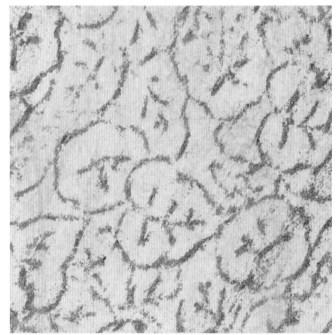

Oil-pastel resist

Enhancements to paste paper using chalks, mica powder, and other media

Use various paints or media for negative mono printing on a black surface.

Lines of Lumin Arte's Radiant Pearls paint (Sources, page 78) were added thickly to the paper and a comb was dragged through the paint on an angle with a wiggle. The colors blended and the mica rose the top, leaving shimmering lines of color.

Opalite inks are interference colors that look white but the shimmering color shows as the light hits the surface.

The technique of negative mono printing can be used on many surfaces. For this example I used a small ceramic tile. The effect is dazzling, and you can use it to create decorative accents for your home.

Ceramic tiles and other premade surfaces can be used for home decor.

When you have just a little paste left in your cup or on your brush, reverse the process and apply the paste directly to the rubber and stamp it on the paper. This way no paste is wasted.

Direct-to-rubber is yet another technique to try.

TIP

If you use LuminArte's Primary Elements or Polished Pigments to add color to your wallpaper paste, you can let the tiny bits of paste left in the cup dry. When the color solidifies, you can peel it out like confetti. If paste is brushed on a tile or Teflon craft mat, you can also peel up the dried paste to use as an accent.

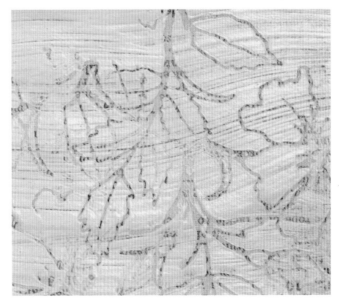

Preprinted paper gives an unusual effect as it shows through when you press the stamp on the surface with paste, then remove the paste.

How much preprinted paper shows through depends on how solid the stamp is.

Chipboard Book: Museum of Memories

This is a project that can be completed in a few hours. Various techniques will be highlighted as options, but the simple collage is a personal statement of the person creating the book.

Supplies

- Mini chipboard book, *You & Me*, School Clips—Karen Foster Designs

- Metal frame, Studio K stickers, die cuts—K&Company

- Tea Dye and Old Paper Distress Inks, Adirondack Pen—Ranger

- Attic Collection stickers, tag, and paper clip—EK Success

- Chipboard *Time Flies*, epoxy stickers—Provo Craft

- Heritage vinyl attachments—Hot Off the Press

- Collage images of Renoir paintings

- 5 pieces of 3½″× 3½″ paste paper

- Dark Hydrangea Papier paint—Plaid

- Fruit Blossoms stamp—Clearsnap

- ½″ Supertape, Memory Tape Runner—Therm O Web

- Scissors

- Small applicator sponge

How-To

1 Mix the hydrangea paint with the paste. Create the cover with paste and mono printing (see page 34) and collage.

2 Make the pages with mono-printed paste paper and collage. Antique some of the stickers with Ranger's Tea Dye ink with a small applicator sponge (used on the watch faces, little sticker words, and *Time Flies* chipboard). Following the manufacturer's instructions, adhere the words *timeless*, *past*, *memories*, and *remember* to Supertape. Remove the protective liner, then stick the words onto the page.

3 Stain the back pages and inside covers with Distress Ink.

Gallery

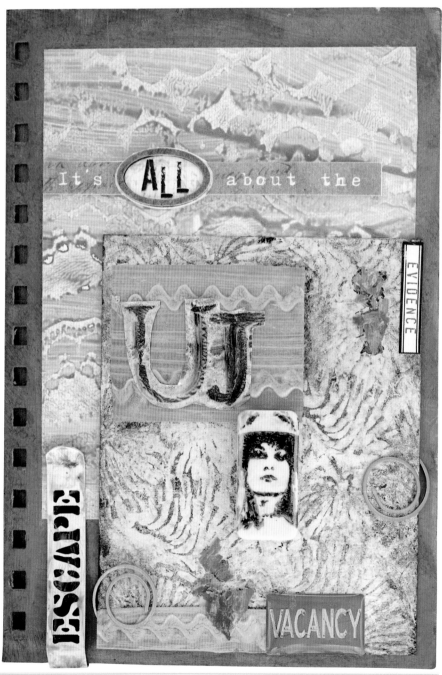

Altered book cover using paste paper—made with a Tsukineko Opalite re-inker (Sources, page 78), stickers, and embellishments

Keepsake necklace made from a mint tin

A nature collage using tile.

Winter Inspiration **journal, which Patty Dennis covered and collaged with paste papers and stamped and inspirational pages**

Patty Dennis used paste paper as a background and layered collage, using a paper punch to punch out shapes in the collage.

Pam Yee stamped over paste paper, cut out a window and attached a photo, and created an inspirational card. An extra strip of paste paper is used as an accent.

Patty also created a simple collage card with ripped paste paper and paper-punched hearts.

A collaged card that Pam created using the direct-to-rubber technique, with paper paste and a brushed paste background

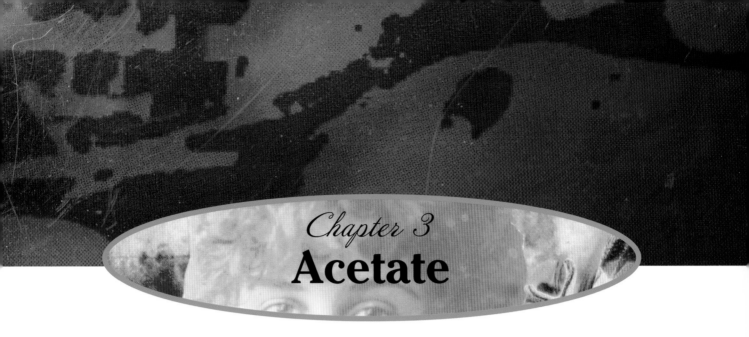

Chapter 3
Acetate
and Clear Materials

A window to the world, clear materials let you see through to the spirit within. Clear materials include acetate, glass, clear laminate, plastic, and so on. Working with clear surfaces is one of my favorite ways to work. You can create both on top of and underneath the surface!

Clear materials tend to be nonporous, which means the media used will not soak into the surface—whatever you use sits on top. This can be a tricky problem, but with today's technology making wondrous products possible, creating beautiful art is fast, fun, and easy!

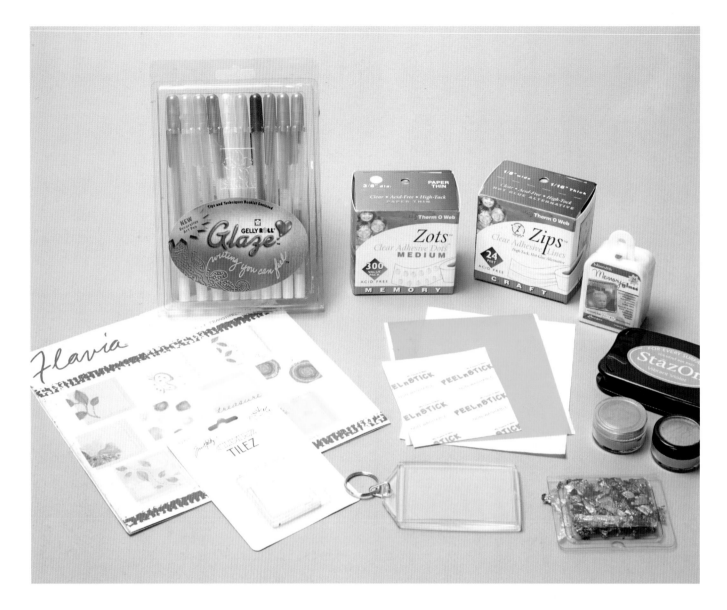

Basic Tools

- Materials such as acetate, clear laminate sheets, plastic, glass, and computer transparency sheets

- Coloring products such as glaze, pens, pigments, and glass paint

- Collage images, papers, and stickers

- Gold leaf—USArtQuest

- Various adhesives such as decoupage medium, double-sided adhesive, and so on

- Microtip scissors—Fiskars

This is my favorite technique! I am infatuated with color and love spending a day creating these stickers to use later.

Mica-Powder Painted Stickers

Supplies

- Matte laminate sheets—Therm O Web

- PeelnStick double-sided adhesive sheets—Therm O Web

- Primary Elements and Polished Pigments powders—LuminArte

- Black StazOn ink—Tsukineko

- Small, pointed watercolor brush

- Microtip scissors—Fiskars

- Texture sponge—USArtQuest

- Rubber stamp of your choice (Use images that are outlines or have an open design.)

How-To

1 Stamp an image on a laminate sheet and let it dry. (Make sure you are stamping on the front of the laminate and not the protective liner.)

2 Peel the protective liner from the back of the laminate sheet, leaving the adhesive face up. Use the protective liner on one end of the exposed sticky side to have a place to put your hand or finger so the laminate sheet doesn't move around.

3 Dip your brush into the mica powder container then tap it off, so you have color on your brush but not too much. Start with the large, open areas, moving the powder until it sticks to the sticky sheet and no excess powder remains. Once you have completed the small areas, continue "painting" in the larger areas. Don't worry if the powder goes outside the stamp's edge; you will be cutting it out. Don't be afraid to mix colors together!

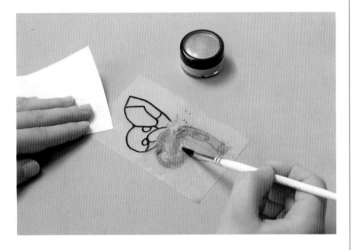

4 For extra dazzle, press gold leaf or glitter in the open areas after painting the powder. Rub it smooth with your finger or a stiff texture sponge.

5 Once you've finished painting the powder on the sticky side of the laminate, cut a piece of double-sided adhesive to the size of the laminate sheet you just painted.

6 Peel 1 protective liner from the double-sided adhesive and press the adhesive to the sticky side of the laminate sheet that was painted with powder. Smooth the sheets together from the center out.

Another mica-powder painted sticker

7 Cut the sticker out following the outline of the stamped image. To use, peel the protective liner from the back of the newly made sticker and stick to artwork.

Perfect Harmony

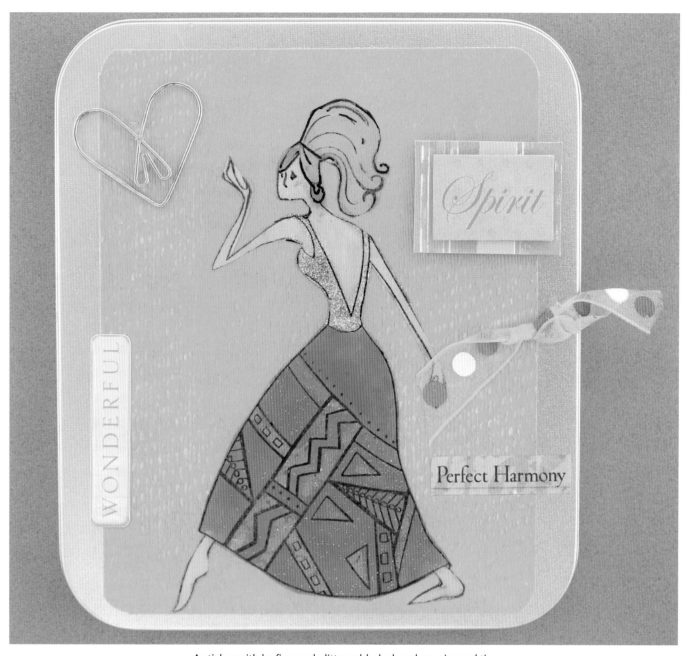

A sticker with leafing and glitter added, placed on a journal tin.

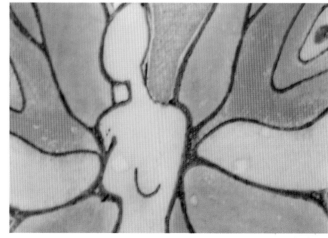

1 Use images that you have stored on your computer or scan your artwork or other images into the computer. Print on the opposite side of the computer transparency sheet than the manufacturer suggests.

2 Place the printed transparency sheet wet side down on cardstock (or smooth watercolor paper or preprinted, patterned paper). Rub the dry side of the transparency (also called burnishing, I use the back of a spoon).

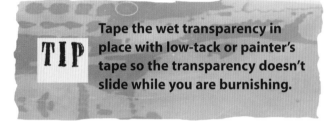

TIP Tape the wet transparency in place with low-tack or painter's tape so the transparency doesn't slide while you are burnishing.

3 Lift up the transparency, and the image is now on the cardstock! Single-color graphics were used in the sample below, but multicolored images will transfer in color.

Ink-Jet Transfer

My printer has a specific way of feeding computer transparency sheets so that when the image is printed, it will dry and not smear. I accidentally put a transparency sheet into the tray upside down, and the ink remained wet on the sheet. Just to see what would happen with my "mistake," I placed the sheet facedown onto cardstock and rubbed the design onto the cardstock. Voilà! A transferred image.

TIP When printing out images be sure to reverse any words (an option on the print program menu) so they don't transfer backward.

Single-color transferred image

Multicolor transferred image

A printed transparency mounted with brads. (Image by ArtChix Studio)

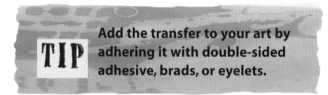

TIP Add the transfer to your art by adhering it with double-sided adhesive, brads, or eyelets.

A transparency adhered with Peel N Stick double-sided adhesive.

Glaze pens on acetate, backed with decorative paste paper (see page 34)

Glaze Pens on Acetate

Glaze pens and Soufflé pens from Sakura of America (Sources, page 78) are wonderful, dimensional inks made specifically for nonporous surfaces. I love to use them on acetate and glass! Simply stamp the outline image onto acetate and then color it in with the pens as you would a design in a coloring book. Sakura's Soufflé pens were designed for black or dark surfaces, but they work just as well on light surfaces.

Embossing-Enamel Transfer

Embossing enamel is thick, and great for making transfers. As an added touch, use a texture sheet (Sources, page 78) to add texture that will show through the transfer.

Supplies

- Clear embossing enamel—Pipe Dreamink Opals
- Suze's Melting Pot—Ranger
- Color photocopy
- Texture sheet—Krafty Lady
- Craft sheet—Ranger
- Bowl of cool water

How-To

1 Pour the embossing enamel into the melting pot and melt the embossing powder following the manufacturer's instructions.

2 Place a color photocopy face up on your craft sheet and pour the melted embossing enamel over the whole image.

3 Immediately press the texture sheet on top of the poured enamel to create a pattern. The texture sheet is pliable and can be lifted off the enamel easily after a few seconds. Let the embossing enamel harden.

TIP Pouring enamel so that it is a "shard" shape (see photo above), gives an unusual effect—like an old piece of cracked pottery or an aged painting. While the enamel is warm, you could also try cutting around the enamel to get the shape you want, or run it through a die-cutting machine with a shaped die.

4 Once the enamel has hardened, place the enameled image into a bowl of water. Let it sit for about 3 minutes.

5 Take the piece out of the water and lightly rub the white coating of the back of the photocopy until all you are left with is the image embedded into the embossing enamel. You may have to soak the piece for another 1–2 minutes if the coating isn't completely removed.

6 Adhere the enamel transfer to any project using multipurpose glue that dries clear.

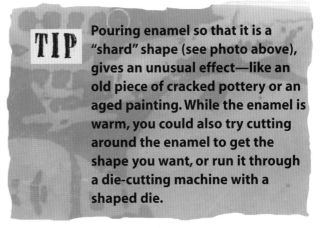

Collage Behind Glass

This is a fun technique in which images are collaged under the glass and embellishments are collaged on top.

Supplies

- Glass coaster
- Decoupage medium—Plaid
- Decorative paper—Durwin Rice
- Colored cardstock
- Vintage woman image—ArtChix Studio
- 12″–15″ of fiber (depends on size of coaster)—Fiber Scraps
- Brass heart lock and key charms—ArtChix Studio
- Miscellaneous stickers
- Designer tacky glue—Aleene's by Duncan
- Foam brush
- Microtip scissors—Fiskars

How-To

1 Cut the cardstock and decorative paper to fit the back of the coaster. Stamp the vintage woman image and cut around the woman's head and upper body to fit in the cardstock circle.

2 Brush the back of the coaster (except the rim) with decoupage medium. It will be milky white when wet but will dry clear. Place the image facedown on the back of the coaster over the decoupage medium, and press into place from the center out, removing any wrinkles.

3 Brush more decoupage medium over the back of the vintage woman image, and on the exposed coaster if needed, and fit the decorative paper facedown over the image. Smooth from the center out to adhere. Do the same with the cardstock piece, fitting it over the decorative paper.

4 Run a line of tacky glue around the outside rim of the coaster. Press the fiber into place and trim off any excess. Let dry.

5 Glue the heart lock and key in place on the front of the coaster. Add stickers to the front of the coaster.

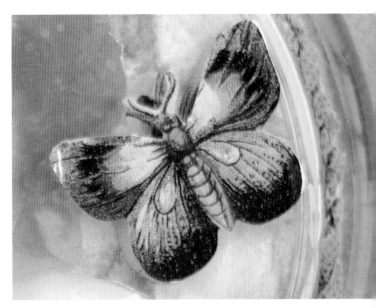

Another example of the collage-behind-glass technique

Gallery

Colored transparency images, rub-ons, and a stamped mirror were used on this blank board book. I colored the stamped image with glaze pens.

A window was cut and a transparency image was adhered from the back of the page.

The inside of this key fob was layered with an image-stamped and computer-printed colored transparency scrapbook sheet; the outside was collaged with part of a cut and printed transparency sheet, and tinted stickers and charms were added.

For her *Floral Shadows* card, Diana used the ink-jet transfer technique with chalk, and wax etched by scratching into the surface.

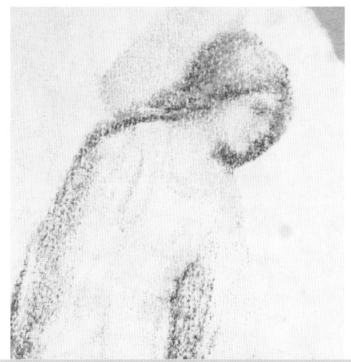

Diana Pernick used the ink-jet transfer technique on her *Angel Guardian* card.

Adhesive-backed sticker stamped with image, adhered on tile, and colored with glaze pens

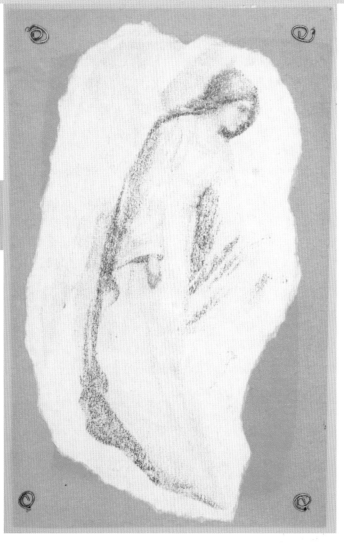

Chapter 4
More Art Techniques

These are techniques I use a lot when playing with collage and mixed-media works of art. Decoupage has been around the art world for years. The collages of the past used shellac as the medium to seal the decoupage in a manner that really gelled the images to look like they had melted together. Shellac is caustic and smells bad, but in the past fifteen years or so other water-based and noncaustic media have become available. Using these safer media I have been able to simulate the same feel that the shellac produced, without worrying about health and safety issues.

Distress-Ink Collage

With memory pages and altered art re-creating looks of faded photos, the distress-ink collage technique fits well with the current trends. A photo that you took today can look vintage by tonight!

Supplies

- Black mat board (size depends on what size collage you want)

- Double-sided adhesive sheet (same size as mat board)

- Collage papers—Plaid

- Tea Dye and Vintage Photo Distress Inks, Glossy Accents medium—Ranger

- Scissors

- Copper gilding leaf, texture sponge—USArtQuest

- Memory Tape Runner—Therm O Web

- Sponge applicator

- Foam brush

How-To

1 Find collage papers that appeal to you and cut out various pieces. (I used the boys as the focal point along with the *Washington Public Schools* and *Butter Milk* captions.)

2 Arrange all the pieces on the mat board to help you decide where you want them to go. Carefully take the pieces off the mat board and set them aside in the same arrangement.

3 Remove the protective liner from one side of the double-sided adhesive sheet. Starting from the bottom of the mat board, press and smooth the adhesive sheet to slowly adhere it, working the adhesive sheet to fit the mat board. Rub the whole mat board smooth with your fingers, moving from the center to the edges.

4 Remove the protective liner from the second side of the adhesive sheet. Be careful, as the surface will be sticky—once something sticks to it, that item is there to stay.

5 Work from the bottom layer of the collage to the top. Start with the collage papers you want in the background and press them into place on the mat board. Keep adding pieces to the collage by pressing them onto the sticky mat board or gluing them to the background pieces.

> **TIP** If a piece of collage paper overlaps where no double-sided adhesive is left exposed, use the tape runner to add adhesive.

6 Once all the pieces are in place, spread gilding leaf over the areas of sticky mat board that are still exposed. Use the texture sponge to rub the gilding leaf onto the surface.

7 With the sponge applicator, pick up some of the Tea Dye distress ink and wipe it over the surface of the collage. Tea Dye is a beautiful, light aging color. Next, wipe some Vintage Photo ink in only a few areas. The Vintage Photo ink is darker, so use it sparingly. These inks will add to the desired vintage look.

Aging the surface with Distress Inks

8 Squirt some Glossy Accents (a 3-D gloss medium) on the surface of the collage. Use a foam brush (or your fingers) and brush the medium over the whole surface, covering the entire collage. Let dry. More gloss medium can be added as needed.

This is a fabulous way to create embellishments that have a cloisonné look, like the leaf and the tag on this piece of art.

"Cloisonné" Embellishments

My friend Doreen and I were experimenting with alcohol inks one day. I asked her what it would look like to use alcohol inks with shrink-art plastic and shrink it down. We tried it, and the finished result looked like cloisonné jewelry! Ranger has developed supplies that make alcohol ink projects easy and less expensive than projects using Pantone inks. I have shown the technique using a heat tool, but a toaster oven (following the package instructions for shrink-art plastic) can be used as an alternative.

Supplies

- White shrink-art plastic—Ranger

- Lettuce, Butterscotch, and Raisin Adirondack alcohol ink—Ranger

- Adirondack alcohol ink applicator and felt pads—Ranger

- Adirondack Blending Solution—Ranger

- Gold Adirondack Mixative—Ranger

- Nonstick craft sheet

- Scissors

- Die-cut machine

- Heat tool

- Paintbrush

- Wood side of a rubber stamp, an acrylic block, or a metal spatula

How-To

1 Place a piece of felt on the alcohol ink applicator. Bring the bottle of Lettuce Adirondack alcohol ink to the felt and squeeze to add ink at both ends of the applicator. Put Butterscotch ink next to the Lettuce ink. Add Raisin ink to the center.

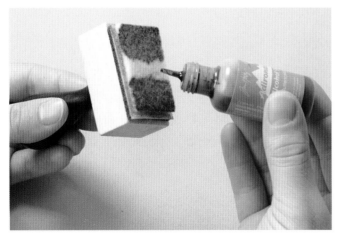

Applying alcohol ink to the felt applicator

TIP Bring the tip of the alcohol ink directly to the felt (instead of squirting close to the felt); it will prevent the alcohol ink from squirting all over and making a mess!

2 Tap the applicator on the shrink plastic, turning the applicator right and left to create a bubbly pattern.

Applying ink to shrink plastic

3 Add a small squirt of blending solution to the felt that is on the applicator. Following the manufacturer's instructions, shake the Adirondack Mixative and add a few drops on top of the blending solution on the felt. Tap the applicator over the shrink plastic where you just applied the alcohol ink. You will notice the ink spreading, causing beautiful golden bubbly patterns on the surface.

4 Once the ink dries, use a die-cut machine to cut shapes out of the shrink plastic. Place one piece at a time on the nonstick craft sheet and use the end of a paintbrush on one corner of the shape to hold the piece in place.

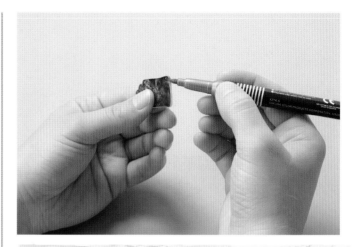

Use a paintbrush to hold the piece in place as it shrinks. Remove the paintbrush to finish the shrinking.

5 Use a heat tool to slowly add heat to the piece. The piece will begin to fold over and look like it will stick together, but a second later it will unfold. Once the shrinking stops, place a spatula or other heavy object over the piece and press down. This will flatten the piece so it doesn't curl while cooling. Once the piece has cooled, you can use it as an embellishment, or to create jewelry!

TIP When you shrink the plastic, the edges will be white. If you like, use a metallic pen to color the edge of the shrunken piece.

The shrink-art plastic before and after it has been heated

kids

DREAM

Gallery

Use a transparency image as an accent.

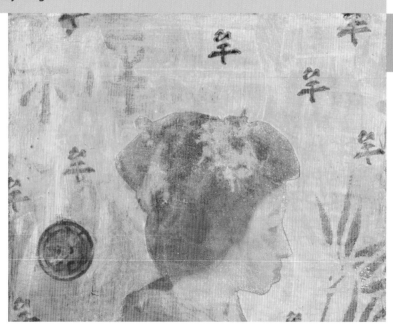

Mat board painted, decoupaged, stamped, and distressed

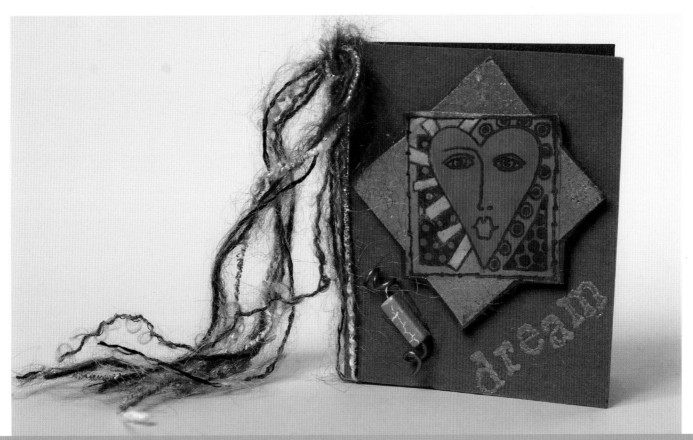

The center accent is laminate sheet

Cardstock collaged on both sides, cut to fit 2 pieces of glass, and sealed with foil tape. Dried leaves are used inside as an accent.

Multilayered tag art using Tsukineko's opaque white StazOn ink

A transparency transferred onto a laminate chip, then collaged on a small wood piece covered with paper

I used transferred transparency images to make this collage piece.

I decoupaged and distressed a cachepot for a unique look.

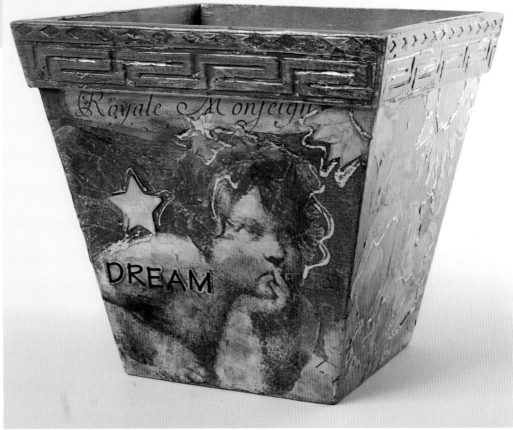

Chapter 5
Creative Color Theory

"Mere color, unspoiled by meaning, and unallied with definite form, can speak to the soul in a thousand different ways."

OSCAR WILDE

When it comes to color, students want to learn how to put colors together harmoniously. Choosing the right color seems an almost magical process, with choices of color depending on whether it "looks good to the eye" or "feels right." Good color harmony attracts the viewer with visual interest.

A simple understanding of the basic ideas of color and color theory can propel artists to new heights of creation, as control of how they want their art to look and feel is achieved. When you understand how to put color and design together, any art form becomes easier.

The Color Wheel and Color Combinations

Sir Isaac Newton developed the first color wheel. The colors within the color wheel represent the foundation colors that are used to create all other colors. There are many color wheels that can be purchased; however, I recommend making your own color wheel if you are first learning about colors.

Primary Colors

The primary colors are red, yellow, and blue. These are the colors that cannot be created by a combination of other colors. These colors provide the basic foundation for color mixing.

Secondary Colors

These are colors that are made by mixing two of the primary colors together, such as green (yellow and blue), orange (red and yellow), and violet (blue and red).

Tertiary Colors

These are colors that are made by mixing a primary color with a secondary color, such as red-orange (red and orange) or green-blue (green and blue).

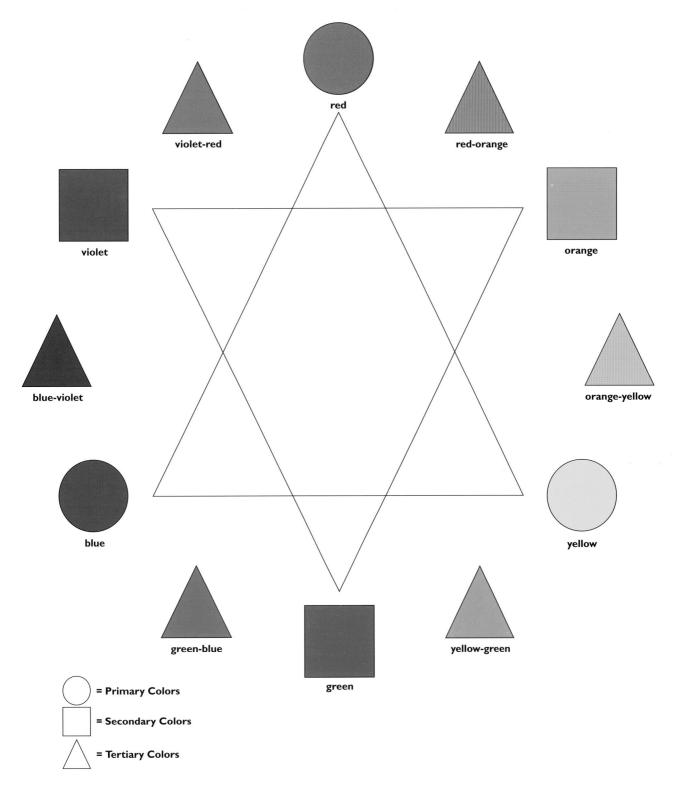

red

violet-red

red-orange

violet

orange

blue-violet

orange-yellow

blue

yellow

green-blue

yellow-green

green

○ = Primary Colors

□ = Secondary Colors

△ = Tertiary Colors

A color wheel with primary, secondary, and tertiary colors.

 TIP Art materials such as paints, chalks, and pastels have pigment of a certain color. When these colors overlap on the art layout, many times a new color will emerge based on what the combination creates.

Color Terminology

- **Hue** A color or a particular gradation of color

- **Shade** Adding black to any color for a darker value

- **Tone** Adding gray to any color for a medium value

- **Tint** Adding white to any color for a lighter value

- **Temperature** Describes whether a color is "warm" or "cool"

Warm colors are usually thought of as the colors of the sun or fire, such as yellow, red, and orange. Warm colors are "active" colors; they excite the viewer and have a more intense value. Cool colors are usually thought of as the colors of the ocean or sky, such as blue or purple. Cool colors are "passive" colors; they relax the viewer and have a less intense value. Green is a "neutral" color, neither warm nor cool.

- **Value** The saturation of the hue/color or the strength of the color

TIP

Make color selection even easier with the Paper Crafter's Color Companion from Create & Treasure! (Sources, page 78)

Color Themes

- **Monochromatic** Hues, tints, and/or shades of the same color

Monochromatic shades of blue

- **Complementary** Two colors directly across from each other on the color wheel

Complementary colors of orange and blue

- **Split Complementary** A color plus the colors on either side of its complement on the color wheel

Split complementary colors of yellow, violet-red, and blue-violet

■ **Triad** Three colors an equal distance from each other on the color wheel

Triad colors of red, yellow, and blue

■ **Analogous** Colors adjacent to each other on the color wheel

Analogous colors of yellow, yellow-green, and green

Easy Theme Color Chart for Primary Colors

Red

Complement Green

Split Complement Green-blue and yellow-green

Triad Blue and yellow

Analogous Violet and violet-red, or red-orange and orange

Yellow

Complement Violet

Split Complement Violet-red and blue-violet

Triad Red and blue

Analogous Orange and orange-yellow, or yellow-green and green

Blue

Complement Orange

Split Complement Orange-yellow and red-orange

Triad Red and yellow

Analogous Green and green-blue, or blue-violet and violet

Color Proportion and Concentration

Colors that are next to each other on a layout cause the eyes to see a particular mix. The mix will depend on the relationship of the color to the chosen area on the layout. In the Focal Point section this concept will be defined in greater detail. When choosing colors, remember that a dominant color with a few semidominant colors and an accent color can create harmony. Use the themes from above to determine which color is dominant, which colors are semidominant, and what would be an appropriate accent color.

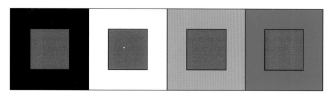

Different backgrounds change the relationship of the red focal point.

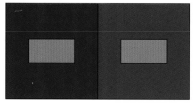

The shade and color of the lavender rectangle appear to change against a blue-violet versus a violet-red background.

Design Definitions

Design incorporates basic elements and techniques that help you create balance and harmony in your work so that it is pleasing to the eye.

Basic Elements of Good Design

Focal Point

The focal point is the element in the layout that the eye is drawn to first. There may be more than one focal point, but more than a few confuse the eye, unless they are equal in size, forming a symmetrical layout. The focal point is usually a large element that is set off by medium and smaller elements.

Alignment

Good alignment creates a strong edge so the eye can follow from one part of the page to another. Usually the alignment starts with the focal point, which is placed to the left or right, or upper or lower part of the layout. Be careful not to put the focal point dead center because the eye will tend not to move to the other elements of the artwork.

Repetition

Choose colors, elements, and accents on your layout to make them look unified on the page. Using the same color, a specific size element, or the same shapes more than once will create harmony in the artwork. Repetition can create movement.

Proximity

The space between elements determines the relationship between the various elements of the artwork. Too much space in a layout can make the work look disconnected, empty, or unharmonious. A work with not enough space can appear chaotic and tends to be hard for the eye to look at.

TIP Plan your layout with a simple sketch (or lay out the pieces of the collage on the surface before gluing them) to help you see the relationship between the elements and space with ease.

More Design Definitions

■ **Lines** Define boundaries and connections in a work

■ **Shape** The characteristic surface configuration of a thing; an outline or contour, or something distinguished from its surroundings by its outline

■ **Value** Light and dark contrast in a particular color

■ **Movement** Direction that moves the viewer's eye around

■ **Pattern** Like texture, visual patterns are created with lines, shapes, and colors

■ **Harmony** Similar elements that evoke serenity and calm

■ **Contrast** Draws attention to the work and keeps it from being boring

■ **Rhythm** Spaces between shapes and colors to create a mood

■ **Balance** Moving the pieces until they are either symmetrical or asymmetrical

■ **Symmetrical** The form on opposite sides of a dividing line is balanced

■ **Asymmetrical** The form on opposite sides of a dividing line is unbalanced

■ **Dominance** Focal point, a main focus

■ **Unity** Results from the successful use of all the above techniques in a finished work

■ **Overlapping/Bridging** Connecting pieces of a design together, either joining two pieces together directly or using a third piece to tie two other pieces together

More Design Options

Embellishments have become extremely popular in creating art. Embellishments are anything used to add dimension or texture, or to enhance a layout. Beads, buttons, fibers, and charms are some of the many embellishments that can be used.

Use inks, paints, and other media to enhance the surface, either before or after other elements are added. Walnut ink, direct-to-paper (adding ink directly from the inkpad to the paper), modeling pastes, and so on all give a certain feel to the layout.

Conclusion

I hope you have enjoyed this journey. Now it's time to jump right in and

play!

Express who you are through your art, following the techniques given.
Once you start playing, you will never want to stop!

After you finish playing for yourself, enjoy creating gifts and RAKs (random acts of kindness) to bring even more happiness to the world!

Sources

7 Gypsies
6049 Slauson Ave.
City of Commerce, CA 90040
323-890-2115
www.7gypsies.com

After Midnight Art Stamps—Lila's Divine Play Images
P.O. Box 830
Laveen, AZ 85339
866-634-9408
www.amstamps.com

All My Memories
12218 S. Lone Peak Pkwy., Suite 101
Draper, UT 84020
888-553-1998
www.allmymemories.com

ArtChix Studio
585 Stornoway Dr.
Victoria, BC V9C 3L1
Canada
250-478-5985
www.artchixstudio.com

Chapel Road Artstamps
5 Invermara Ct., Unit 1
Orillia, ON L3V 8B4
Canada
705-329-0130
www.chapelroadartstamps.com

Clearsnap
P.O. Box 98
Anacortes, WA 98221
360-293-6634
www.clearsnap.com

Colorbök
2716 Baker Rd.
Dexter, MI 48130
800-366-4660
www.colorbok.com

Create & Treasure
1651 Challenge Drive
Concord, CA 94520
800-284-1114
www.createandtreasure.com

Design Originals/Art Papers
2425 Cullen St.
Fort Worth, TX 76107
817-877-0067
www.d-originals.com

Duncan Enterprises
5673 E. Shields Ave.
Fresno, CA 93727
559-291-4444
www.duncancrafts.com

Durwin Rice
5516 Troost Ave.
Kansas City, MO 64110
800-304-8766
www.durwinrice.com

EK Success
125 Entin Rd.
Clifton, NJ 07014
973-458-0092
www.eksuccess.com

Ellison/Sizzix
25862 Commercentre Dr.
Lake Forest, CA 92630
949-598-8822
www.ellison.com

Fiber Scraps
82 Windover Ln.
Doylestown, PA 18901
215-230-4409
www.fiberscraps.com

Fiskars
7811 W. Stewart Ave.
Wausau, WI 54401
715-842-2091
www.fiskars.com

Hero Arts
1343 Powell St.
Emeryville, CA 94608
510-652-6055
www.heroarts.com

Hot Off the Press
1250 N.W. 3rd Ave.
Canby, OR 97013
800-227-9595
www.paperwishes.com

Hot Potatoes
2805 Columbine Pl.
Nashville, TN 37204
615-269-8002
www.hotpotatoes.com

Impression Obsession
P.O. Box 5415
Williamsburg, VA 23188
757-259-0905
www.impression-obsession.com

Junkitz
17 Sweetmans Ln., Bldg. #12
Manalapan, NJ 07726
732-792-1108
www.junkitz.com

K&Company/Studio K
8500 N.W. River Park Dr. #136
Parkville, MO 65152
816-389-4150
www.kandcompany.com

Karen Foster Design
623 North 1250 West
Centerville, UT 84014
801-451-9779
www.karenfosterdesign.com

Krafty Lady Art Moulds/R&P Clear Stamps
Rear 9 Edgewood Rd.
Dandenong, VIC 3175
Australia
(+61) 3 9794 6064
www.kraftylady.com.au
(U.S. Distributor: After Midnight
Art Stamps: www.amstamps.com)

LuminArte
3322 W. Sussex Way
Fresno, CA 93722
559-229-1544
www.luminarteinc.com

Mrs. Grossman's Stickers
3810 Cypress Dr.
Petaluma, CA 94954
707-763-1700
www.mrsgrossmans.com

Papers by Catherine
11328 S. Post Oak Rd. #108
Houston, TX 77035
713-723 3334
www.papersbycatherine.com

Paula Best
507 Trail Dr.
Moss Landing, CA 95039
831-632-0587
www.paulabest.com

Pipedream Ink/Opals Embossing Enamel
184 Deep Creek Rd.
Wynyard, TAS 7325
Australia
(+61) 04 0967 1547
www.pipedreamink.com
(U.S. Distributor: After Midnight
Art Stamps: www.amstamps.com)

Plaid Enterprises
3225 Westech Dr.
Norcross, GA 30092
678-291-8100
www.plaidonline.com

Prima Marketing
5564 Edison Ave.
Chino, CA 91710
909-627-5532
www.primamarketinginc.com

Provo Craft
151 East 3450 North
Spanish Fork, UT 84660
801-794-9061
www.provocraft.com

Ranger Industries
15 Park Rd.
Tinton Falls, NJ 07724
732-389-3535
www.rangerink.com

Sakura of America
30780 San Clemente St.
Hayward, CA 94544
510-475-8880
www.sakuraofamerica.com
www.gellyroll.com

Sandi Oberton's Rubber Nature Stamps
8034 335th St.
Burlington, WI 53105
262-694-4058
www.rubbernature.com

Sparkle N Sprinkle
P.O. Box 5767
Ruskin, FL 33571
888-901-9173
www.sparklensprinkle.com

Spellbinder/Wizard
2717 W. Cheery Lynn Rd.
Phoenix, AZ 85017
888-547-0400
www.spellbinders.us

Stampendous
1240 N. Red Gum Ave.
Anaheim, CA 92806
714-688-0288
www.stampendous.com

A Stamp in the Hand
2057 S. Belshaw Ave.
Carson, CA 90746
310-884-9700
www.astampinthehand.com

Therm O Web Adhesives
770 Glenn Ave.
Wheeling, IL 60090
800-323-0799
www.thermoweb.com

Tsukineko
17640 N.E. 65th St.
Redmond, WA 98052
www.tsukineko.com

USArtQuest
7800 Ann Arbor Rd.
Grass Lake, MI 49240
800-200-7848
www.usartquest.com

Xyron
15820 N. 84th St.
Scottsdale, AZ 85260
480-315-2783
www.xyron.com

Zim Prints
340 Rocky Hill Way
Bolivar, TN 38008
731-659-2368
www.zimprints.com

About the Author

A certified professional demonstrator and teacher, Lea works as a freelance designer, demo artist, instructor, and design consultant for several companies in the hobby industry.

Lea's work can be seen in many paper arts magazines and in Design Original and C&T Publishing books. Lea's journey led her to creating stamp images (through After Midnight Art Stamps) to give artists the freedom to create a very personal form of self-expression. See more of Lea's artwork at www.picturetrail.com/LeaC.